have you ever…

*Questions about You, Your Friends,
and Your World*

have you
you
ever...

Questions about You, Your Friends,
and Your World

Bret Nicholaus and Paul Lowrie

Ballantine Books • *New York*

A Ballantine Book
Published by The Ballantine Publishing Group

Copyright © 1999 by Bret Nicholaus and Paul Lowrie

www.randomhouse.com/BB/

LIBRARY OF CONGRESS CATALOGING-IN-PUBLICATION DATA
Nicholaus, Bret.
Have you ever— : questions about you, your friends, and your
world / by Bret Nicholaus & Paul Lowrie.
p. cm.
ISBN 0-345-41760-7 (alk. paper)
1. Conversation. 2. Questioning. I. Lowrie, Paul. II. Title.
BJ2121.N53   1999
302.3'46—dc21
99-31404
CIP

Text design by Debbie Glasserman
Interior illustrations courtesy of Randy Bray

Manufactured in the United States of America

First Edition: November 1999

10 9 8 7 6 5 4 3 2 1

welcome

It is often said that life's a journey. Indeed, each and every one of us has taken a different path that has shaped the person we are and the life we live. Some of us have been here, others there; some of us have done this while others have done that; one of us has accomplished one thing while somebody else has achieved another.

With limited time in our lives, we can't possibly do it all; but most of us enjoy hearing from someone who *has* experienced something that we have only dreamed of doing. What was it like? How did it feel? How nervous were you? Truthfully, few of us can raise our hands in a group and say that we've rafted the Colorado River. But for those of us who haven't, it can be a lot of fun to learn about the road—or river—not taken.

Yet somewhere along life's highway our paths

have converged. We have shared the same experience, done the same thing, been to the same place. Discovering that another person shares a part of who we are brings about a sense of connectedness . . . as well as a wonderful opportunity for great conversation! Let's be honest: It's fun to talk with someone else who, like ourselves, went through the experience of locking the keys in the car. We value common ground.

Have You Ever . . . is a collection of 450 questions that gives you the opportunity to discover what others have done and how their lives differ or equate with your own. At the same time, it affords each of us the chance to talk about ourselves, to "brag" a little. All the questions have been carefully designed to be entertaining and noncontroversial; you can feel comfortable using our book with family, friends, children . . . even people you've just met.

In addition to learning about others, you'll learn a lot about who *you* are in the process of perusing this book. What have you done that you had forgotten about? What haven't you done that you still hope to accomplish? You'll uncover the answers to these and many other questions as you weave your way through the thought-provoking pages of *Have You Ever . . .*

Some suggestions for playing *Have You Ever . . .* are on pages 1 to 3.

a special note to our readers

None of the questions in this book has been created to be an end in itself; rather, each query is designed to serve as a jumping-off point for further conversation. For example, instead of simply answering "no" to question #29 and moving on, pause for a moment . . . and think about the types of silly mishaps that *have* happened to you. Soon you'll be talking about the time you slammed your finger in the door or dropped that heavy box on your foot. For question #6, don't dismiss the question if you haven't spent an October in Vermont; instead, talk about that spring azalea festival you experienced in the South, or the memorable snowy Christmas you spent at Vail. *Have You Ever . . .* should *always* be used to enhance your conversations, not restrict them!

have you ever . . .
as a fun group game

Have You Ever . . . is a great icebreaker game and source of entertainment that will get people of all ages mixing, mingling, and having fun in no time. There are many ways to enjoy *Have You Ever . . .* Here are our favorites:

1. *For any size group, large or small.*

Gather everyone together in a central location in a room. Read a *Have You?* question aloud. Every person who can honestly answer "yes" to the question moves to the right side of the room; all "noes" shift to the left side of the room.

Read another question from the book. All "yes" responses move (or stay) to the right side; all "no" responses move (or stay) to the left side.

As you continue to read different questions, the

two groups will continually change, getting larger or smaller depending on each person's response. Plan on reading about 20 questions; this will allow enough time for some fun interaction and virtually ensures that each player will find that he/she has something in common with every other participant.

2. For groups of 10 or more.

In advance of the gathering, choose any 16 questions that you really like from the book. With a pen (or a computer), divide a standard-size sheet of paper into 16 squares (much like a bingo card). Write/type one *Have You Ever . . .* question in each square and then make enough copies so every guest can have a sheet. (If your group is large enough and you so desire, it's OK to make several different playing sheets, each containing different questions.) Provide a pencil or pen for each player.

Give the participants about 10 to 15 minutes to mingle, asking one another the questions on the sheet. The "asker" should continue reading questions aloud until the "respondent" finally answers "yes" to one. At that point, the respondent puts his/her signature in that question's square and cannot—at the moment—be asked another question. (The respondent may, however, become the asker at this point; this efficiently allows each party the chance to fill a square on his/her sheet with the other person's name.) After each of the other participants has at least been solicited for a "yes" response to one of the questions, the asker may go back to anyone else and try to secure another "yes" to an unsigned question. *The goal of the game is to get each of the 16 squares signed.* (*Note:* Each participant may himself/herself sign off on one square, provided a "yes" response can honestly be given to a question.) In rare instances, there may be a square that nobody can honestly answer. That's OK; it shows that everyone in the group has something in common!

In theory, the winner is the first person to get a signature in each of the 16 squares; however, it's far more enjoyable for everyone else if the winner is left unannounced and each participant continues to ask around until all of his/her squares are signed or the time limit expires.

1

Have you ever been to Disney World?

2

Have you ever blown a tire
while driving?

3

Have you ever flown in something other than an airplane?

4

Have you ever met a professional athlete?

5

Have you ever called in sick when you weren't really sick?

6

Have you ever been in New England during autumn?

7

Have you ever refused to pay for a meal at a restaurant?

8

Have you ever served on a jury?

9

Have you ever been inside a castle?

10

Have you ever been in a restaurant and discovered something in your food that shouldn't have been there?

11

Have you ever had anything published?

12

Have you ever taken a peek at someone else's diary?

13

Have you ever had the chicken pox?

14

Have you ever helped to stop a crime?

15

Have you ever been on a Caribbean cruise?

16

Have you ever lost your wallet?

17

Have you ever broken a bone?

18

Have you ever memorized the Gettysburg Address?

19

Have you ever played in a band?

20

Have you ever been stuck in an elevator?

21

Have you ever worked on a farm?

22

Have you ever been chased by a dog?

23

Have you ever run out of gas
while driving?

24

Have you ever caught
a ball in the stands
at a professional baseball game?

25

Have you ever been stung by a bee?

26

Have you ever been to Alaska?

27

Have you ever "adopted" a grandma or grandpa (e.g., someone at a nursing home, an older person in your neighborhood, etc.)?

28

Have you ever won money in a lottery?

29

Have you ever hit your thumb with a hammer?

30

Have you ever looked at a map just for the fun of looking at a map?

31

Have you ever complained at your local post office about poor mail delivery?

32

Have you ever fallen asleep during a sermon?

33

Have you ever ridden a motorcycle?

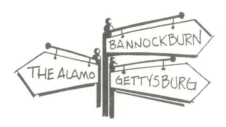

34

Have you ever visited a famous battlefield?

35

Have you ever been to the Grand Canyon?

36

Have you ever literally X'd off the days on a calendar in anticipation of something?

37

Have you ever met a professional musician?

38

Have you ever been so happy you cried?

39

Have you ever lost an important piece of jewelry?

40

Have you ever eaten some kind of exotic, wild game?

41

Have you ever gone ice fishing?

42

Have you ever marched in a parade?

43

Have you ever accomplished something that everyone else told you would be impossible to achieve?

44

Have you ever locked your keys in the car?

45

Have you ever eaten at a famous restaurant?

46

Have you ever seen something so beautiful it nearly took your breath away?

47

Have you ever witnessed a
natural phenomenon?

48

Have you ever thanked the person
who had the greatest influence
on your life?

49

Have you ever left your Christmas
tree up past January 15?

50

Have you ever been to a wedding
where the bride/groom
changed her/his mind?

51

Have you ever been in
Minnesota in January?

52

Have you ever been written up
in the newspaper?

53

Have you ever slammed a
door on your finger?

54

Have you ever been locked out
of your home?

55

Have you ever had a pen pal?

56

Have you ever gone on a blind date?

57

Have you ever mistaken a person for someone else?

58

Have you ever completely forgotten where you parked the car?

59

Have you ever predicted something that ultimately did happen?

60

Have you ever enthusiastically said "yes" to something you wish you had adamantly said "no" to?

61

Have you ever had a hole-in-one?

62

Have you ever attended a class reunion?

63

Have you ever been told you look like someone famous?

64

Have you ever learned a foreign language?

65

Have you ever seen an endangered species (or other rarely seen animal) in the wild?

66

Have you ever lied about your age?

67

Have you ever climbed a mountain?

68

Have you ever gotten lost in a big city?

69

Have you ever started
your own business?

70

Have you ever been to a state fair?

71

Have you ever traveled abroad?

72

Have you ever known or met someone over 100 years old?

73

Have you ever found more than $10 lying on the ground?

74

Have you ever gone whale-watching off the coast?

75

Have you ever walked out of a theater because the movie was so bad?

76

Have you ever milked a cow by hand?

77

Have you ever had your picture taken with someone famous?

78

Have you ever been stranded at the airport?

79

Have you ever suffered from poison ivy?

80

Have you ever researched your family's history?

81

Have you ever played a trick on a friend?

82

Have you ever personally met someone who was at least seven feet tall?

83

Have you ever saved someone else's life?

84

Have you ever counted up the number of hours you've been alive?

85

Have you ever made a citizen's arrest?

86

Have you ever been in a play?

87

Have you ever read a book that you literally couldn't put down?

88

Have you ever experienced a blizzard?

89

Have you ever driven more than 1,000 miles in one day?

90

Have you ever thrown caution to the wind and done something totally outrageous?

91

Have you ever experienced a natural disaster?

92

Have you ever been on television?

93

Have you ever been thrown a surprise party?

94

Have you ever accidentally ruined a surprise for someone else?

95

Have you ever invented, created, or developed a new product?

96

Have you ever enjoyed a movie at the theater so much that you went back to see it again within a couple of days?

97

Have you ever done volunteer work in your community?

98

Have you ever tried a food you thought you'd hate but ended up liking?

99

Have you ever spent a weekend at a bed-and-breakfast?

100

Have you ever read a famous American's autobiography?

101

Have you ever read the entire New Testament of the Bible?

102

Have you ever written out your long-term goals?

103

Have you ever hosted a foreign visitor in your home?

104

Have you ever eaten an entire lemon (the pulp) by itself?

105

Have you ever knowingly committed a traffic violation when nobody was around?

106

Have you ever started a major project that you never finished?

107

Have you ever skipped work or school to watch a major news event on TV?

108

Have you ever pretended to be someone that you aren't?

109

Have you ever held a political seat at any level?

110

Have you ever had a pet besides a dog or cat?

111

Have you ever visited a national park?

112

Have you ever had a severe sunburn?

113

Have you ever won a contest?

114

Have you ever fasted?

115

Have you ever walked or driven across a famous bridge?

116

Have you ever declined a promotion?

117

Have you ever bought something you thought you'd love, only to regret the purchase soon thereafter?

118

Have you ever taught a class?

119

Have you ever been to Hawaii?

120

Have you ever been to a circus?

121

Have you ever tried to get out of jury duty?

122

Have you ever provided Christmas gifts for a needy family?

123

Have you ever filed a complaint with the Better Business Bureau?

124

Have you ever donated blood?

125

Have you ever hit a deer while driving?

126

Have you ever wondered what was really behind the JFK assassination?

127

Have you ever been to the Everglades?

128

Have you ever made a prank phone call?

129

Have you ever written a letter to the president of the United States?

130

Have you ever sung in a choir?

131

Have you ever traveled a long distance on foot?

132

Have you ever been so upset with a product that you willfully destroyed it?

133

Have you ever ridden on a "highest" or "fastest" roller coaster?

134

Have you ever jumped in a rain puddle just for the fun of it?

135

Have you ever met a descendant of a famous American?

136

Have you ever worked in retail sales?

137

Have you ever driven the same car more than 150,000 miles?

138

Have you ever been pleased with your driver's license photo?

139

Have you ever heard an organ concert in a large cathedral?

140

Have you ever walked away a winner in Las Vegas?

141

Have you ever had a startling encounter with a wild animal?

142

Have you ever gone white-water rafting?

143

Have you ever waited in a line for more than one hour?

144

Have you ever witnessed a national news event?

145

Have you ever scored the winning point in a sporting event?

146

Have you ever ridden an animal besides a horse?

147

Have you ever visited the birthplace of a U.S. president?

148

Have you ever struck up an enjoyable conversation with a total stranger?

149

Have you ever fainted?

150

Have you ever witnessed lightning striking something?

151

Have you ever extended a vacation because you were having so much fun?

152

Have you ever been audited by the IRS?

153

Have you ever attended the Olympic Games?

154

Have you ever seen a ghost?

155

Have you ever followed through on a New Year's resolution?

156

Have you ever been a victim of a household mishap?

157

Have you ever invited a chef or gourmet cook over for dinner?

158

Have you ever taken a scenic train ride?

159

Have you ever fallen asleep at work?

160

Have you ever coached a sports team?

161

Have you ever spilled something very hot on yourself?

162

Have you ever visited Washington, D.C.?

163

Have you ever found something suspicious-looking?

164

Have you ever swum with a dolphin?

165

Have you ever snuck a peek in someone else's closets or medicine cabinet?

166

Have you ever met anyone who fought in a battle?

167

Have you ever bought something from a bakery or store and then claimed that you made it from scratch?

168

Have you ever spent the Fourth of July in a historic town?

169

Have you ever taken an IQ test?

170

Have you ever wished you had chosen a different career?

171

Have you ever forgotten something really important?

172

Have you ever gone more than 24 hours without any sleep?

173

Have you ever bought something you didn't really need just so you could keep up with the Joneses?

174

Have you ever found a rare coin in your pocket change?

175

Have you ever been to New York City?

176

Have you ever built something from scratch?

177

Have you ever thought about furthering your education?

178

Have you ever listened in on a private conversation?

179

Have you ever demanded a raise?

180

Have you ever taken a really unusual tour?

181

Have you ever purposely taken a walk in the rain?

182

Have you ever ordered a pizza with everything on it?

183

Have you ever done something considered extremely dangerous?

184

Have you ever delivered a speech to a large group of people?

185

Have you ever refused to tip a waiter or waitress?

186

Have you ever been on a hayride?

187

Have you ever paged through a dictionary just for fun?

188

Have you ever driven a vehicle faster than 100 miles per hour?

189

Have you ever been swimming in the ocean and suddenly discovered that a shark was in the vicinity?

190

Have you ever avoided doing something because of a superstition?

191

Have you ever lost your luggage on a trip?

192

Have you ever been on the radio?

193

Have you ever kept a diary?

194

Have you ever had your picture taken in front of a state's WELCOME sign?

195

Have you ever danced under the stars?

196

Have you ever been frostbitten?

197

Have you ever wanted to travel back in time?

198

Have you ever had a scary experience onboard a plane?

199

Have you ever used a limousine service for a special occasion?

200

Have you ever sent flowers to someone for no special reason?

201

Have you ever felt that a prayer of yours was truly answered?

202

Have you ever attached a message to a helium balloon and sent it off?

203

Have you ever gone more than three months without weighing yourself?

204

Have you ever thought that you would make a good actor/actress?

205

Have you ever talked your way out of a speeding ticket?

206

Have you ever refused to pay a bill you received in the mail?

207

Have you ever had an unwanted creature—like a mouse— in your house?

208

Have you ever pinned or taped up a great quotation so that you would be reminded of it daily?

209

Have you ever gone around railroad gates that were down in order to beat an oncoming train?

210

Have you ever taken a winter walk in the woods?

211

Have you ever hidden something in such a great spot that you couldn't find it when you needed it?

212

Have you ever bowled higher than 250 in a single game?

213

Have you ever gone through a hardship that ultimately made you a stronger person?

214

Have you ever been addicted to a television show?

215

Have you ever read the same book three times or more?

216

Have you ever laughed so hard you cried?

217

Have you ever made something worse by trying to fix it yourself?

218

Have you ever served as a consultant for anything?

219

Have you ever watched an Elvis Presley movie from start to finish?

220

Have you ever hitchhiked?

221

Have you ever made a major career change?

222

Have you ever had a professional massage?

223

Have you ever been in a crowd larger than 100,000 people?

224

Have you ever invited a pastor or priest to your house for dinner?

225

Have you ever thought seriously about writing a book?

226

Have you ever gone at least one full week without watching TV?

227

Have you ever thrown something away that later you wished you hadn't?

228

Have you ever had a vacation ruined because of inclement weather?

229

Have you ever owned a convertible?

230

Have you ever experienced déjà vu?

231

Have you ever been in New Orleans during Mardi Gras?

232

Have you ever heard a sermon so good
that you can't forget it?

233

Have you ever given someone a gift that
was originally given to
you by someone else?

234

Have you ever, as an adult,
slept with a stuffed animal?

235

Have you ever memorized
the Bill of Rights?

236

Have you ever experienced a spiritual awakening in your life?

237

Have you ever been camping in the wilderness?

238

Have you ever been deep-sea fishing?

239

Have you ever experienced an ethnic tradition besides one of your own?

240

Have you ever bought an entire CD just for one song?

241

Have you ever done in-depth research on a particular topic?

242

Have you ever rewarded yourself for a job well done?

243

Have you ever gotten reacquainted with a long-lost friend?

244

Have you ever thought about going into the ministry?

245

Have you ever discovered the secret to something?

246

Have you ever bought the videotape of a classic movie?

247

Have you ever been involved in an accident in a parking lot?

248

Have you ever watched the sun rise or set on a lake or ocean?

249

Have you ever been caught up in a fad?

250

Have you ever found a vacation spot you liked so much that you return to it again and again?

251

Have you ever taken a class that ended up being a total waste of your time?

252

Have you ever been bitten by a pet, either your own or someone else's?

253

Have you ever played a famous golf course?

254

Have you ever held a live snake in your hands?

255

Have you ever spent the night sleeping on a beach?

256

Have you ever literally waited for the mail carrier to deliver an important letter or package?

257

Have you ever thought about changing your name?

258

Have you ever lived in a town with a population of less than 3,000?

259

Have you ever wondered what heaven is like?

260

Have you ever been on a safari?

261

Have you ever worn braces on your teeth?

262

Have you ever been to a rodeo?

263

Have you ever gotten up in the middle of the night to make a snack for yourself?

264

Have you ever taken the scenic route rather than the main highway on a trip?

265

Have you ever sent or received a piece of fan mail?

266

Have you ever served in the armed forces?

267

Have you ever withheld your opinion on a serious topic in order to avoid a major argument?

268

Have you ever been to the top floor of a skyscraper or other tall structure?

269

Have you ever done something that at one time you said you'd never do?

270

Have you ever invested in a stock that skyrocketed for you?

271

Have you ever turned an age that you didn't want to turn?

272

Have you ever started a club or small group?

273

Have you ever wanted to live in a different part of the country?

274

Have you ever been part of a progressive dinner?

275

Have you ever made snowballs and preserved them in the freezer?

276

Have you ever been caught doing something really funny on home video?

277

Have you ever splurged on something you normally wouldn't?

278

Have you ever been so hot that you thought you might collapse?

279

Have you ever met anyone who worked for the CIA or FBI?

280

Have you ever had a cooking "disaster"?

281

Have you ever hit your head so hard on something that you saw "stars"?

282

Have you ever been a season-ticket holder for anything?

283?

Have you ever been to a restaurant where they offered a prize for eating all of something?

284

Have you ever hailed a taxi?

285

Have you ever gone shell collecting on a beach?

286

Have you ever been at a complete loss for words?

287

Have you ever gotten an electric shock you'll never forget?

288

Have you ever lied about the size of a fish that you caught?

289

Have you ever been transferred somewhere that you didn't want to go?

290

Have you ever tried to find the oldest tombstone in a cemetery?

291

Have you ever explored a cave?

292

Have you ever gotten sick from an amusement park ride?

293

Have you ever been in attendance for a professional championship game?

294

Have you ever been sick from food poisoning?

295

Have you ever been totally enthralled by a TV miniseries?

296

Have you ever spent the night at a hotel at which you wish you hadn't?

297

Have you ever narrowly avoided a very serious accident?

298

Have you ever subscribed to a magazine for more than 10 years in a row?

299

Have you ever participated in an activity that you thought you'd hate but ended up liking?

300

Have you ever read a #1 New York Times best-selling book?

301

Have you ever been unable to balance your checkbook?

302

Have you ever experienced a flood in your home?

303

Have you ever driven from coast to coast?

304

Have you ever been unable to stop sneezing?

305

Have you ever water-skied?

306

Have you ever walked on the field/court of a major sports stadium?

307

Have you ever, as an adult, bought a child's toy for yourself?

308

Have you ever lost your patience with a store's sales associate?

309

Have you ever followed a path just to see where it led?

310

Have you ever embarrassed yourself while trying to make a good first impression?

311

Have you ever visited a location where a major motion picture was shot?

312

Have you ever accidentally broken something that didn't belong to you?

313

Have you ever gotten lost—or lost someone else—in a crowd?

314

Have you ever gone swimming where a NO SWIMMING sign was posted?

315

Have you ever stopped to help someone stranded on the side of the road?

316

Have you ever been to Minnesota's Mall of America?

317

Have you ever dozed off while driving a car?

318

Have you ever driven the same car for more than 10 years?

319

Have you ever taken a stress test?

320

Have you ever spent Christmas in Colonial Williamsburg?

321

Have you ever had something in your house destroyed by a pet?

322

Have you ever met someone with a truly unique talent?

323

Have you ever worn your hair dramatically different from the way it is now?

324

Have you ever been in your state's capitol building?

325

Have you ever started something that became a tradition for you?

326

Have you ever seen a battle reenactment?

327

Have you ever been a best man or maid of honor in a wedding?

328

Have you ever been on an island?

329

Have you ever visited or driven through a town that looked like an ideal place to live?

330

Have you ever been caught in a deluge of rain with nowhere to hide?

331

Have you ever added up approximately how much money you've made up to this point in your life?

332

Have you ever overcome a fear of something?

333

Have you ever eaten in a restaurant that rotates?

334

Have you ever bought an *original* of something?

335

Have you ever lost a great opportunity because you were a few minutes too late?

336

Have you ever been somewhere so remote that you lost all sense of civilization?

337

Have you ever taken a horse-drawn carriage ride?

338

Have you ever met anyone who looked or sounded like someone famous?

339

Have you ever thought about where you'd like to retire?

340

Have you ever experienced a summer so wonderful that you didn't want it to end?

341

Have you ever received the red-carpet treatment for something?

342

Have you ever been to a graduation, wedding, or other festive event where something went hilariously wrong?

343

Have you ever participated in a community-improvement project?

344

Have you ever met a stranger on a vacation who ultimately became a good friend?

345

Have you ever been made an offer that you just couldn't refuse?

346

Have you ever had a really bad case of the hiccups?

347

Have you ever taken a taste test?

348

Have you ever, as an adult, done anything really fun with a large group of kids?

349

Have you ever had a computer disaster?

350

Have you ever learned how to play chess?

351

Have you ever been to a gala event for a select few?

352

Have you ever personally known (or at least met) identical twins?

353

Have you ever read something really powerful in a book that keeps coming back to you?

354

Have you ever performed a solo?

355

Have you ever received an award or special recognition for outstanding work or service on the job?

356

Have you ever sat next to someone really obnoxious at a public event?

357

Have you ever been to a small-town festival?

358

Have you ever stuck your foot in your mouth (figuratively speaking) in a major way?

359

Have you ever taken up an unusual hobby?

360

Have you ever dreamed in color?

361

Have you ever traveled historic Route 66?

362

Have you ever carried something around with you for good luck?

363

Have you ever skied a black-diamond run?

364

Have you ever watched a movie solely for the special effects?

365

Have you ever been persuaded to buy something from an infomercial?

366

Have you ever been on a battleship?

367

Have you ever solved a mind-boggling puzzle?

368

Have you ever seen hail as big as golf balls?

369

Have you ever discovered something interesting buried in the ground, or in the attic or wall of an old house?

370

Have you ever been to an air show?

371

Have you ever seen the Northern Lights?

372

Have you ever literally fallen into something?

373

Have you ever bought something from a salesperson who came to your door?

374

Have you ever boisterously rooted for the away team in the midst of a home crowd?

375

Have you ever missed a great photo opportunity because you didn't have your camera?

376

Have you ever had a nickname?

377

Have you ever been exceptionally nervous about meeting someone?

378

Have you ever driven through West Virginia?

379

Have you ever put a coin on the train tracks?

380

Have you ever heard a song that made a lasting impression on you?

381

Have you ever spoken with an older person with the express intent of learning about the past?

382

Have you ever driven through the night to get somewhere?

383

Have you ever received life-changing advice from someone?

384

Have you ever done something unique on your birthday?

385

Have you ever known or met someone who was born on February 29?

386

Have you ever cut yourself so badly that you needed stitches?

387

Have you ever dreamed you were in an airplane that was about to crash?

388

Have you ever spent the night in a creepy, old house?

389

Have you ever ordered a flaming dessert for two?

390

Have you ever seen a painting that you wish you could step into?

391

Have you ever watched the same movie more than 10 times?

392

Have you ever heard a sports commentator call a play that was so exciting it gives you goose bumps just thinking about it?

393

Have you ever been conned into doing something?

394

Have you ever missed out on something special because you were sick?

395

Have you ever been without a major utility for more than 48 hours?

396

Have you ever had your car stolen?

397

Have you ever tried to give someone a good scare just for fun?

398

Have you ever received a really bad haircut?

399

Have you ever done something that most people would consider boring that for you was the thrill of a lifetime?

400

Have you ever been in a large public crowd and by chance spotted someone you knew among all the strangers?

401

Have you ever played Cupid, bringing two people together who eventually got married?

402

Have you ever suffered from insomnia?

403

Have you ever served as an extra in a movie?

404

Have you ever seen a famous person out of his/her element (e.g., a professional athlete shopping at the mall)?

405

Have you ever gotten sick on a food and been unable to eat it ever since?

406

Have you ever gotten into a fistfight with a friend?

407

Have you ever broken up a fight between two other people?

408

Have you ever taken piano lessons?

409

Have you ever fallen asleep in the bathtub or shower?

410

Have you ever had a brand-new car damaged in an accident?

411

Have you ever been enamored of a TV show's theme song?

412

Have you ever been scared stiff by a horror movie?

413

Have you ever accidentally washed
something very important
down the drain?

414

Have you ever been the sorry victim
of a mosquito feeding frenzy?

415

Have you ever learned sign language?

416

Have you ever moved more than
twice in one year?

417

Have you ever lied to someone about how much money you make?

418

Have you ever engaged in a pillow fight as an adult?

419

Have you ever given yourself a complete haircut?

420

Have you ever purposely left the price tag on someone's gift?

421

Have you ever been emotionally devastated by a national or international news event?

422

Have you ever pulled over to the side of the road simply to admire a magnificent view?

423

Have you ever lost or accidentally thrown away an important document?

424

Have you ever had a really annoying neighbor?

425

Have you ever been to summer camp?

426

Have you ever been in a situation where you felt totally out of place?

427

Have you ever attended an annual stockholders' meeting?

428

Have you ever known someone with a really funny name?

429

Have you ever been to Graceland?

430

Have you ever been told that you look younger than your age?

431

Have you ever driven through a state that you couldn't wait to get out of?

432

Have you ever snuck your own food or drink into a theater, sports stadium, or restaurant?

433

Have you ever experienced a recurring dream?

434

Have you ever gone swimming outside when the air temperature was below 32 degrees Fahrenheit?

435

Have you ever "had it out" with a boss?

436

Have you ever had an excruciating toothache?

437

Have you ever had a cavity drilled and filled without taking Novocaine (or any other painkiller)?

438

Have you ever done anything mischievous, but harmless, just for fun?

439

Have you ever been talking with someone only to discover that you have a mutual friend?

440

Have you ever stood on the Continental Divide or other famous line of demarcation?

441

Have you ever taken an ice-cold shower?

442

Have you ever been so proud of something you did that you felt like you could burst?

443

Have you ever been to a Broadway musical?

444

Have you ever encountered a salesperson who simply wouldn't leave you alone?

445

Have you ever driven around your town trying to pick out your "dream house"?

446

Have you ever helped an injured animal that didn't belong to you?

447

Have you ever nicked or dented a parked car and then driven away without leaving a note?

448

Have you ever been seasick?

449

Have you ever radically changed your original opinion or viewpoint on a major issue?

450

Have you ever made a "top ten" list of the most exciting things you've ever done?

a note to our readers

Please write to us at the address below and let us know how you are using the book or what your favorite questions are. As always, we would love to hear from you, and thanks again for including us in your conversations!

Paul Lowrie and Bret Nicholaus
P.O. Box 340
Yankton, SD 57078

about the authors

Bret Nicholaus and Paul Lowrie received their degrees in public relations/advertising and marketing, respectively, from Bethel College, St. Paul, Minnesota. They have collaborated on four popular previous books: *The Conversation Piece, The Christmas Conversation Piece, The Mom and Dad Conversation Piece,* and *Think Twice!*. They are full-time writers, publishing consultants, and product developers. Here are their answers to a few questions from this book. Go back and find the question that fits the answer and you'll learn more about Bret and Paul.

Bret's answers:

#1   "Yes, twelve times. In my opinion, it's the greatest vacation spot in the world. Thanks, Walt!"

#61   "On a 165-yard par 3. It landed on the

front of the green, rolled slowly toward the hole, and dropped in. I remember being in a daze for about 30 seconds. There were four witnesses."

#297 "I was riding in a car that slid on a patch of ice on the interstate and was struck by an eighteen-wheeler going 55 miles per hour. The car was totaled, but miraculously the driver, two other passengers, and I walked out without any serious injuries."

Paul's answers:

#35 "The first time I saw it, I was part of an Easter sunrise service there. As the sun slowly rose, the canyon became visible a little bit at a time. If a picture is worth a thousand words, that sight was worth a million!"

#371 "Yes, in Minnesota, but something even more impressive was a meteor I saw north of Los Angeles. Streaking slowly across the sky, it showered sparks like a huge fireworks explosion.

An incredible green glow remained for about five or six seconds."

#383 "A professor in college made the statement 'People don't fail, they just quit.' This quote has inspired me ever since, and especially helped me never to give up on our very first book, *The Conversation Piece.*"